MAFIA PROFESSOR JEON (Mafia)

Calypso Everdeen

Contents

Chapter 1

Y/n introduction.Name: y/n kim .AGE: 19: From South korea.Bestfriend: Lisa .She is from rich family her father is biggest buisnessman in the world.

Jeon Jungkook.AGE:26 From south korea.He is mafia but he wants to become professor he wants to teach people about nature and he is professor of Seoul big unniversity. Bestfriend:7 Mafia bestfriendKnow as BTS. Rm.jin.suga.jhope.jimin.tae.jk .

{#1. Y/n wake up u lazy girl' Her mom was waking her up cuz it's her first day in university today eomma pls only 2min said y/n Aniyo get up I'm coming in 5min wake up and get ready if u don't get ready I will give u one tight slap in ur cheek wake upppp!!!!!Y/n mom leave the room.Y/n pov;Ahhhh!! I wanted too sleep but I have to get ready it's my first day in university yaahhhh! Let me call Lisa . Yahh! Why this gurl not accepting my call .Why Lisa sent this mgs:In chatLisa: heyy babe I'm mgs u cuz my phone have 2 % left so I mgs u and gett ready for university it's our first day I'm going to get ready u get ready first okk quickly get readyY/n:okkk byyEnd of chat Y/n quickly got ready and it's her outfit:

~Y/n had her breakfast. And went to university.Lisa outfit:

Lisa:ok let's gooo I'm excitedY/n Mee tooo!Beel ring!Y/n: Lisa let's gooo in classThey gone to there class so first lecture is math everyone is waiting for teachers.Lisa:why is teacher not came yet?Y/n: teacher will come wait Lisa:mmm...*One girl : the teacher is very handsome and cuteNext girl':yess I wanna see him from my eyes I can't wait.Lisa: ahh! Thoes gurl are irritating. Y/n:mmmm lisaaa lookkkk over there!!Every one in classroom looking too teacher anddee the teacher issss???Jeon Jungkook Lisa: OMG he iss soooooo hotttttttt Y/n:yes .. hi students I'm ur math teacher I hope u will study well (cold tone)Jk outfit:

Chapter 2

He loThan he started teaching .....After sometime jk phone rings.

Jk : students I'm coming don't make noise ...

Lisa: yah he is so hottt I wish he was not my teacher ....Y/n it's ok Lisa Lisa don't u like him ?Y/n I didn't say I don't like him he is really handsome and cute but he is cold so I have no interest in him .Lisa are u serious y/n Y/n yess I'm serious.

(They were talking and that time jk came (*hehe Surry)

Jk : why u two are talking didn't I said don't talk now get ready for punishment.(He said cold and agry glancing at u two.)*Y/n sir we are sorry pls .Jk u think I will let u go after saying sorry to me Lisa sir we are really sorry we didn't mean to talk.Y/n sir can't u give us second chance sir pls......Jk :fine but don't do again.

Lisa thanuuu sirrr .Y/n thanku.Jk, mmm ..i know it's short but u don't even comment I feel like ghost is looking ?

Chapter 3

Beel ring=

Y/n ' finally time to go home today was not gud day..Lisa 'yes Mr Jeon shouldn't have say that much to us we were just talking....Y/n' let it be rose let's goo ..Y/n at home*She is now scolding her phoneHer mom had called her Y/n 'why is mom now calling me let me see In living room*Yes mom what?Y/n mom ' y/n can u go and buy some vegetables I need for tomorrow my friend are commenting to visit us .Y/n' oh ok I will go let me change my outfit...Y/n outfit:

Y/n mom ' go safely ok Y/n 'yes mom don't worry byy....In m arket.Y/n 'ok aunty how much total?Aunty ' 200* Y/n 'ok by auntyAunty'by go safely........In road way to home.I was watching my phone than suddenly bumbed to someone??' watch or u goo !!Y/n' omg sorry(*Bowed)??' it's ok let's go Jungkook(* Wait

Jungkook my professor)*??Y/n' OMG sir it's u I didn't know sir I'm sorryJk' u should watch where u goingY/n mind *" he is so hot handsome he is looking cute in casual outfit..Jk' are u listening me y/n?Y/n 'oh yess sir! Jk' where u coming from oh market.Y/n' yes Sir I should get going my mom must be worried about me Jk'mm by go safely or u want me to come to u with ur houseY/n 'noo sir it's okk ok byy sir ....??: Jk who is she

Chapter 4

??: Who is she Jk;. My student. (Guys let be clear the man asked is v ok I don't wanna keep suspen) V: ohh she was scared while talking to u Jk: mmmm maybe let's goo .Y/n pov^I got home and I had my dinner now I'm trying to sleep but I was thinking about Mr Jeon like I don't know what is going own Y/n'; what is wrong with me he is my professor nothing else let me sleep...

Next day:Your outfit~

Y/n mom; y/n bright is here come fast.Y/n: bright is hereee.....*~ Run run ~In living room

Bright; hieeee y/n Bright outfit~~

Y/n : how are u ???Bright: fine I'm back from Thailand since I was missing u I can't even think anything without u Y/n mom

: something something?Y/n; eoma we are bestfriend nothing is going on right brightBright; I don't think so Y/n: (she was looking him like he did something)Bright; aunty no we are bestfriend nothing is going on Y/n mom: ok ok u two talk I'm going in my room I have something to do while u had breakfast?Bright; aunty yes Y/n : eoma I'm going by I'm late I will eat my breakfast there byY/n mom; ok by Bright; let's go I will go to ur university let's see how it is Y/n ; let's go (They were going but she bumbed with someone)??; Why u are always bumbing Mee do u have eyes

Chapter 5

Y/n;? Mr Jeon OMG! I'm really sorry sir I didn't see u coming in really sorry....Jk; u have to open ur eyes and go u stupid girl.....(Jk was about to walk but bright hold his collar)Bright; who the fuck are u u don't know how to talk with girls?!??Jk; mind ur words u don't know me Bright; I don't wanna know u are just a useless man who doesn't respect girlsJk; u who the fu- Y/n; shut up both of u bright he is my professor mr Jeon and nothing happened let's go bright(Y/n was about to walk but Jungkook hold her wrist)Jk; oh now u have boyfriend in university I thought u are a innocent girl just come and study but no u are oppositeBright; I don't care if u her Professor or something if u talk like that with y/n I'm telling don't ruin ur life.Jk; omg I'm scared (he comes closer to bright) and said (- u should don't talk with someone u don't know and for better u should take ur gf or mind will happen somethingY/n; bright let's goo (she takes him forced)Bright; just wait and watch u bastarJk; hah

Chapter 6

Y/n; pov Y/n; bright I don't wanna go today university let's go homeBright; are u scared of this ur professor will do something?!Y/n; noo ! I am not scared just I wanna go home-Bright;ok let's go.(Suddenly bright phone rings)Bright; yes..Ok ! Ok yes I will be there in a min Bright; y/n I have to go it's some imergency ok I will call u later ok go carefully ok mgs me by Y/n; by..Today is bad day I will just go home and watch Kd. -(While waking someone hold her wrist.)Y/n; hey !! Leave me ??; stup up u are the one who fight in morning with mr Jeon Jungkook right?Y/n; it was not A fight some misunderstanding. But who the f*ck are u?????; oh I forgot to introduce myself I'm kim taehyung Jungkook bestfriend.Y/n; oh I think I have saw u somewhereTae:yes at night u were waking and bumbed with Jungkook. U are so childish.Y/n; yahh! Don't call me childishI have to go Tae: sure see u soon miss kim Y/n; what I'm y/n not miss kim and don't cross ur limit ok Tae; ok ok by go carefull y.(Tae left) In y/n house ; Y/m; y/n go get ready my friends are coming for dinner ok Y/n; mmm.. Y/n outfit;

Y/m; y/n come down guests are here

..Wait waitMr Jeon Jungkook and kim taehyung !!!!!!!!!!!!!!!!!!!

Y/n; what are u doing in my house?!Y/m; ohh y/n they are my friend child kim taehyung and Jeon Jungkook. Y/m; meet my daughter y/n .Jk; yes I know her very well she study in the same university and I'm professor of her .Tae; yes I know her twoo we'll right miss y/n?Y/n; y-ess (Why u stutters why I didn't do anything)Tae; wait let me introduce to someone my bestfriend Jungkook fiance.Y/n: f-iance mr Jeon u are committed.? Jk; yes miss y/n . Why are u suprise? Y/n; nono ! I didn't mean that way Tae: miss Olivia come .

Olivia

Olivia; hie y/n I'm Olivia Jeon sooon to be Jeon right Jungkook .Jk; yess oliY/n; hi nice to meet u

Chapter 7

Y/n; nice to meet u

Olivia; u are so beautiful and cute and u are Jungkook's students so it's really good to meet u

Y/n; thanku miss Olivia.Tae; so miss y/n we are here to invite u to Jungkook as weeding.Y/m : yes kim taehyung we will come but my husband is not here he is in China for some business so we can come but he can't I hope u don't mind. Tae; no mam it's ok Jk; yes mam don't worry. Y/m ; why Jeon Jungkook and kim taehyung here mom are not here u know they are my bestfriend why didn't they come Jk; oh I'm sorry I forgot to say that mom is in newyork for some important work and taehyung mom also gone with my mom that's why we come here..Y/m; oh ok no problem and u have to stay here if u say no I will never talk to u both Jk; no aunty pls don't say like that we will stay here Y/m; good. Y/n show there room I am going to kitchen to make lunch ok Y/n ; oh ok eomma (She showed guest room one room Jungkook and taehyung will stay and another room will stay Olivia) Now I'm in my room thinking something but don't know how to explain..... Y/m ; y/n come down lunch is ready call Jungkook and Olivia Taehyung is in downstairs. Y/n; I knocked the door but still no response again but no response in doorI opened and the next scene is really. Ewwwwwww ,

Olivia is kissing him and Jungkook is holding her waist I coughThey become stock Olivia; don't u know y/n to knock on someone room while getting it without permission.(Said with a silent voice not rude ok/) Y/n; I have knocked so many times and called ur names but there were nooo response so I get in I didn't know that u two were doing this I don't have any interest of watching this and emoma said that lunch is ready so I came here to say .(I left) Olivia; it was so awkward I'm going to eat ik hurgy let's go kokieJk;mmm let's go

Chapter 8

(they were having there lunchSuddenly someone came and who could be bright)

Y/m: bright son come have lunch u come in right time and see who come Bright; aunty who are they (Eyes on jk angry stares) Y/m; it's Jeon Jungkook and kim taehyung and it's Jungkook fiance Olivia Jeon Bright; oh nice to meet u guys Tae; nice to meet u man Jk; hi Olivia; hey nice to meet u Bright: hi everyone (Took seat next to y/n) Y/n: where did u go suddenly?! Bright; u know I go to one of my friend house he wanted to propose his crush so I was there helping him How are u ? (Sounds serious) Y/n: fine what about u Bright; no- Tae; hey bright let's her eat she must be hungry right misss kim oh sorry I mean y/n ... Bright; yup y/n we will talk later. Y/n; eat u are looking so tired it will give u energy.......(They all had there lunch and y/n mom is in her room and jk tae bright Olivia and me are in garden)

Olivia; kookie let's go watch movie guys u can join us it will be awesome Bright; y/n u wanna watch movie Y/n; sure like we don't have anything to do Jk; y/n exam are coming don't u wanna study? Y/n; sir professor Jeon I will study afterwards so now I want to watch movie so I will watch any problem mr Jeon Jungkook Jk; no I don't have any problem since u are my student soo just I told Bright; y/n knows what to do no need tell her Tae; ok ok no need to fight let's go

Chapter 9

Next day

Y/n room'|= call to lalisa Y/n; hi Lisa what u doing Lisa; watching kd what u doing? Y/n; u know who is staying at our house?!Lisa; I'm not ghost how can I know speak clearly u stupid ass!! Y/n; fine! Mr Jeon JungkookWaitt;!! Don't shout I am telling u Cuz my mom bestfriend son is Jeon Jungkook I didn't know about it I saw them tomorrow mom introduced me with them I was shocked like how but now it's fine! But!!Lisa; speak ittt!!!! Y/n; mr Jeon have fiance!!! Lisa; hat no u are joking right (Cute ton) Y/n; why I would joke Olivia Jeon ur kd promise Lisa; what are u serious fu*k He is committed, whyyyyy God???????? Y/n; yup I was shockedShe is really beautiful she match with mr Jeon Jungkook they looks beautiful with each other Lisa; mmm whatever ok by take care byy! Y/n; by

(Living room) Y/m is in market). Now only they are together in living room ^ (pew pew) Tae; it's soo boring Jk; yup Y/n: guys I'm going to my roomExcuse me. Tae; wait what u are gonna doo there sit with us let's guys know each other nicely... Jk; yup y/n Y/n; ok guy's as u sayOlivia; y/n so u have boyfriend? Y/n; no Jk; than who is that guy Y/n; his name his bright he is tailand we were friends since childhood we are bestfriend Tae; oh ok that's why he is so touchy with u Nevermind. Y/n; yup mr kim taehyung we are bestfriend aren't bestfriend should be together? Olivia; yup she is right

Chapter 10

Time skip. (Night)Ym: y/n they are going for walk go with themYn: ok In park-Tae; y/n what happened u didn't even watch the movieYn: nothing I was triedTae;oh okI was walking suddenly someone came and hold my hand.

??: liltle one it's late what u doing here. Said in his serious Voice

Who could it be?????Hint: it's not Jungkook or bright ok

Chapter 11

??:Liltle one what u doing here it's late said in is serious tone .

Y/n pov.Wait! Wait! He is the biggest mafia in underworld!Does he know me?

Jk: who are u ??; does it matter to u

V: hey bruh who are u

??: her future husband.

Chapter 12

??: Her future husbandSaid in Deep voice.

Y/n,; are u Vincenzo the mafia of Russia?!

Vincenzo; yes sunshineSaid in serious tone.

Jk; hey do u even know me He shouted

Vincenzo,; yup I know u Jeon Jungkook the underworld mafia-said in serious tone.

Jk; get lost

Vincenzo; really Jeon Jungkook! said laughing.

Chapter 13

Vincenzo;ok let me make it clear I saw her from the first day I like her and her father is my father bestfriend so Jeon Jungkook why are u professor while u are a mafia any reason?Jk; my choice whatever I do Vincenzo don't u look at her with those fucking eye.Vincenzo: Jeon don't u forget you have your fiance . Said smirkedJk; don't cross your limitsVincenzo; fuck you Jeon JungkookSaid pointing a gun to jk

Y/n : please noo ! No! Don't kill him please Vincenzo I said holding Vincenzo shoulder.

Vincenzo; "sunshine "don't cry my love.Y/n; please don't do it.I said crying.Vincenzo; my sunshine ok I will not kill him .said moving my gun .

Chapter 14

Vincenzo= sunshine I'm going to be your future husband so don't make any sense of this Y/n= how can u say who I'm going to marry Vincenzo I don't care about who are u I said shouting.Vincenzo= sunshine let's see who is going to expect the fact.

Chapter 15

Time skip to home.Y/n home:Y/m; y/n open your door S houted.Y/n: I don't wanna marry Vincenzo mom I can decide my life.

Y/m: I know I'm not forcing u ok let your dad come and see what happens ok my y/n now please open your door Y/n ; mom call dad now I wanna talk to him Y/m; ok I'm calling him

Time skip to night y/n dad arrived.Y/m ; y/n look ur dad have arrived open your door

Y/n open the door she walked to her dad her dad was sitting in couch and Vincenzo too.Y/d; y/n i know u have become older enough to make your decision but.He is my bestfriend son we have been in mafia since we were in school I can't say no to him .Y/n; dad u know right I don't wanna marry why u are forcing me I said crying.

Y/m; y/n dad try to understand she doesn't wanna marry him why u are forcing her

Y/d; u know right I promise him that our daughter will marry Vincenzo what is the difference Vincenzo is a powerful mafia and dangerous what u want moreY/n dad shouted.

Vincenzo; y/n sunshine be ready.

Y/n : get the fucking lost from here u idiot. I shouted.

Chapter 16

Y/n pov : It's been 2 week seen I saw my professor Jeon Jungkook he is busy and his fiance is in holidayWhile something's not good with me sometimes I think about what is gonna happen or it is my imagination I don't know?

Lisa: y/n what happened to u since Vincenzo leave that day why are u behaving like that?

Y/n; Lisa u know my father has promised hus bestfriend that I'm gonna marry is son Vincenzo but u know right I don't wanna marry him

Lisa; I know but it's ok we can find solutions about this alrightShe said holding my hand

Y/n pov I cried. I can't hold it back since I meet Vincenzo he ruin my life.

Attention!!!!!Guys I have edit long episode but it became short due to problem I'm sorry guys please don't lose hope on me

Lisa; y/n please don't cry please y/nnieee She said holding my hand

Y/n pov;I was going to answer but someone knocked on the door (I'm in Lisa house).

Chapter 17

Y/n povI was going to answer but someone knocked on the door (I am in Lisa house)

Lisa: who is it She walked to the door opening

Y/n pov It's Jeon Jungkook!Why! Why he is here what the hell is going on!?

Lisa: sir Jungkook what are u doing here do u need some help Said bowing her head.

Jk walked to me .Said=. Miss y/n if u don't mind can I have a word with u

Y/n pov:Whyy meee? Whyy???

Jk ,y/n walked to balconyMeanwhile Lisa is sitting in couch thinking what Jeon Jungkook why he is here .

Y/n: yes sir what u wanna talk Said looking outside of the balcony.

Jk: the day since we met Vincenzo I know what happened ur dad promise hus bestfriend that is son Vincenzo will marry u I know everything so Your mother told me to look after u take care of ur and your parents are going to meet Vincenzo parents to convince them that u are not gonna marry Vincenzo I hope they understand.

Y/n: they didn't even told me and why I have to stay with u I don't wanna stay with u Said walking to door but! Jungkook pull me closer to him !!

Autor pov:(! Why I'm screaming while writing this!)

Jk: y/n it's final u are going to stay with me it's final Said pulling me closer.

Y/n : no why would I .

Jk: your parents told me to take care of ur and I'm going to do that .No matter what happened!

Y/n: fineCan u leave now .

Jk pulled away and walked to downstairs

Lisa; sir what happened

Jk; y/n is coming in my house (Jk explain everything)

(! Pov your autor is lasy yes I'm lasy!?)

Lisa: yes sir u don't have to tension she is coming in 30 mins sir don't worry

Jk: i better not.

Time skipTo Jeon Jungkook house=

Jk: it's your room do whatever u want. But don't go anywhere without me ok And last thing I guess u know I'm a mafia if someone comes here don't leave the door stay in the door alright?

Y/n: fine.

Jk walked to his room.

Chapter 19

Time skip...

Y/n pov=I have been in my room for 2 hoursLet me just take a look of this houseAnd where is this Jeon Jungkook idiotLet me see.Y/n open the door she walked to downstairsIt was 8 pm .Light were off she walked to the light board to light onn when she clicked the switch......!!Jeon Jungkook was inform of her fac e.!!

Y/n pov;My eyes were going to full offf he is standing inform of me 0!

Jk: my dear y/n what u doing here didn't I tell u not to come Said in depp, serious voice.

Y/n: I ----wasss---- just !!I was hungry so I thought to call u but u were not thereI said looking down.

Jk: ok

Time skip to dinner (10pm)

Y/n ; Jungkook sir it's too much I can't eat so much

Jk: u said u were hungry rightGo on eat Said watching u.

Y/n pov=Why I said I was hungry?I'm so idiot now I have to eat 10 dish Take me home,.....

Jk: eat .Said walking to couchJk; and some of my friend is coming here ok Don't be scared.

Y/n: why would I I don't scared by anyoneI said with eating kimchi

Jk pov :She eat like a pig.

Time skip.

Arrived of.fffff????

Chapter 19

Time skip

jk and y/n were sitting in couch waiting for the guest.....

Jk: y/n u know those people one is my friend and one is actor.Y/n: Do I care? I said smriked

Jk: smirkedOk y/n

Time skip.....to(11:30pm)(Door knocked)

Jk: I think they are here

(Y/n immediately sit nicely)

Jk:SmirkedNow u care ?

Y/n: idiot (mumbled)

The door open and it's??Guys I want u guys to guse I'm really serious i give u full hind now u guess ok???

Chapter 20

??:

Jk open the door and it's.

Jk:Welcome iu and tae

Y/n povWhyy this idiot tae come and who is this girl iuWhy do I care

Jk : we have someone's here It's y/n

Tae: Mrs kim u are here Said winking.

Jk: yah tae can u be quite

Tae: rolled eye's.

Pov.They walked to couchY/n is sitting with jk and tae and iu sitting together like 2 sofa are there alright.

Iu: it's been a long time we are togetherSaid drinking water.

Jk: yup after a long mission.

Tae: bytheway what is y/n doing? Here. Said winking to y/n

Jk: (explained everything)I'm lazy seriously I'm lazy.

Y/n: I hope everything becomes normal.

Jk: it will don't worry.

Iu: hi y/n I'm iu BTS members I'm a mafia tooo don't worry u are like my liltle sisterSaid smiling.

Y/n: hi iu UnnieSaid smiling

Tae :guy's let's watch movie

Jk: yup like we have no works to do yup let's watch it

Iu: let's watch "the summer I turned preety"l

Y/n: yes .

Tae: ok let's gooo (They have cinema in there house oki)

Time skip=°

(It's 1:30 am)

Tae : y/n are u ok why are u crying.

Y/ n: it's so sad she like that boy but what about him Said crying

(Suddenly jk hug y/n)

(Heheeeeeeeeeee)

Y/n pov :Jeon Jungkook idiot hug me why ? I don't know but let me just cry and hug him

Jk pov : Y/n hug me tightlyI have to take care of her after what happened

Chapter 21

Time skip to 2 days.

Y/n POV: It's been a while staying here iu Unnie come here and stay with me and idiot Jungkook is good towards me nowadays.

Jk pov:Y/n have been nice those days and today Olivia is coming HERE.

Y/n povI was in kitchen and Jungkookshii come towards me and said

Jk: y/n today is Olivia coming

Y/n: o-h oh

Jk was about to say something but the doorbell rang.

Walk;;;Jk povI opened the door and it's y/n Family!

Y/m: oh Jungkook we didn't told u that we were coming here

Jk:Aniyo its ok uncle aunty.

Come inside please

They walked inside.

Y/d: where is our daughter

Jk: she is in kitchen i guess she is coming

Y/n povJungkook idiot where is the su------

MOM DAD !!!

Y/n run to her parents.

Y/n hug her mom dad tightly

Y/n And her parents talked

(And the main news is the mafia Vincenzo is not marrying Y/N!!!!!

The Bell rang and it'sOlivia.

Olivia hug Jungkook.

Olivia: uncle and aunty tomorrow is our engagement me and Jungkook!!!!

Chapter 22

Time skip to next MORNINGPovY/n are in there house cuz y/n family came and Jungkook is in his house and Olivia has arrived(Disgusting Olivia NVM)

In venu

Y/n and there family are sitting there.

But they didn't know that the karma is picking up them

(NVM cuz u know it u want it guys)

Jk outfit

Jk was standing in the venueBut they Didn'tHaveTheIDEA!!!!!

ThatThatThatThat that I like that baby(Sorry guys i wrote pshy and suga song)

(Ok in the story)

Y/n ': Where is this Olivia Unnie

Y/m': Yah where is she I guess let me go and see her

Y/n: can I come too eoma ?

Y/m: ok

They knocked the doorNo answerAgainNo answer

Y/n : why she is not opening the door

Y/m pushed to door it' opened But She was not THERE.

She left a piece of paperWritten something.

Hi Jungkook i know I did wrong but I was cheating on u i didn't know what to say but I can't put this drama on I'm tried of this I'm not going to marry u And u wanna know whom I'm marryingThe Vincenzo who wanted to married u/n now see how i make her life miserable.

Oliva|

POVY/m was shocked really shocked what to do now no idea she has now

Chapter 23

POVY/m was shocked what to do now she was being scared of losing her daughter and the people waiting there in the venue for Jungkook marriage but OlivaIsNotHere

(The problem we all wanted)

Y/n POV: I was here reading the letter again and again! No idea Why it included me why me ?!

Y/n- mom w-hat are we gonna do now I said shuttering, worried.

Y/m- i h--ave no idea .

Y/m:POVWhat im gonna do now i have no idea wait.!Let me say to Jungkook parents first yah yes .

Y/m- y/n u stay here alright I'm going to call Jungkook parents ok I said holding her hand.

Y/n nod .

IN VENU.Jungkook parents were talking with the guest.

Y/m povI walked to them i said to them and they were shocked!. Her mom was worried scared about the media and the people.

(Cuz they are buisness people popular)

Y/m-Mrs Jeon i have no idea what to do

Mrs Jeon: miss kim i have one i--dea

Mr jeon - darling what it is

Mrs Jeon - if y/n and Jungkook get married She said nervously

Mr Jeon - it is a good idea but miss kim are u sure about this.

Y/m POVY/n and Jungkook marriage!But I have no ways to do now yes Jungkook and my daughter marriage yes.

Y/m-Ok mr Jeon

Chapter 24

Y/mOk mrjeon..Y/n POV I'm sitting in the room my mom told she is coming but where is she Like always my life is hard i--Someone Knocked On The Door

Y/n slowly walked and open the door And it's her Mom and Jungkook parents.

Y/n- mom i said hugging her tightly Mom what will happen no-wY/m couldn't help she cried Mrs jeon - Y/n daughter she said holding her hand Can u please do something for us and for your mother y/n Daughter.She said

Y/n- Y--es aunty

Mr Jeon -Y/n daughter can u marry jung-kook He said nervously

Y/m- my y/n please say yes u know right ur mother always choose good for u right please listen to your mom

Y/n POV -ME marry to that idiot man Jeon JUNGKOOK (yah u are)

Mr Jeon -Daughter Jungkook is nice guy But I hope u know He is mafia and he will always protect u no matter what And i hope Jungkook didn't told u right

Y/n nod.

Mrs jeon -Daughter Are u gonna marry Jungkook YesOr n-o

Chapter 25

Y/nSaid Ye-s anuty I said nervously not knowing what my future holds.Mr Jeon -y/n daughter thanks for ur help Darling get her ready for the wedding Mrs jeon nod Y/m- me Jeon does Jungkook know about this Mr jeon -No he doesn't miss y/m but we have no time to let him know Mrs jeon -Ok we will get her rea-dy

Mr jeon walked away from there.Y/m and Mrs jeon are thereY/n-M--om u think it will be alright Y/m my princess it will be alright okY/n nod Y/n outfit -

Y/m-Omo u look so beautiful my princess Said hugging her.Mr Jeon - I'm really happy to see my son future is really gorgeous I made a right choice

Y/n POV I don't know what is going in but the moment I didn't really expect. To marry Jungkook my PROFESSOR and a MAFIA

In THE VeNu.

Chapter 26

She walked inside the venueHer Heartbeat was on top She couldn't say or think of anything she is like a pice of paper walking there like the air touched her .

Y/m was standing beside the guse and Jungkook parents were standing there But Jungkook was talking with taehyung he was in angry mood like he can kill someone Whoever And Whoever.

Taehyung POV I was talking with Jungkook that one of our mafia member got killed and we don't know who it is but whoever it is he will fucking die from my hand.But!What I see the Jungkook soon to be wife is coming but the veil is there so I couldn't see her face but whatever I don't care.But Someday I will marry y/n I'm sure for it

The priest come and stand between us

The priest said -

-jungkook yes I do .

The priest said to y/n

I---do y/n said

The priest u may kiss the bride.

Y/n POV -Noo omg noooooo idiot Jeon Jungkook nooooo u idiot.She was saying in her head.

Jungkook pov -

I slowly opened the veil in her face But DIDN'T KNOW THAT IT IS Y/N Not Oliva!!!!But why she is marring me Y/n pov The first time I have seen him stocked and the NEXt movement I see his father come towards him he said something.

Jungkook POV

My dad come towards me he said Jd,-, son -i know u are thinking what is going on why y/n is here in Olivia place

I shoot my angry eyes observing what he says

Jd- Jungkook there are many guests and my mafia friends don't put me down and she is a really good girl she is a pure soul Jungkook u understand me

Jungkook pov -I have nothing to say now inform of millions people i nod my head

Y/n pov

He is coming Near me and he hold my neck He peck my lips!!!(, ahhhhhhh ur autor is dieying while writing this)

He whisper in my ear His hot breath touch my skin

He said Don't know where it will lead us but u will leave soon liltle princess.

He peck my lips again

And soon the guest came to congratulate us.

Chapter 27

Soon the guest came to congratulate usThe time to go to the mansion.

Y/n-E-oma i will mi--ss u U said crying Y/m hugged u Y/m-Y/n my baby don't cry i will be always with u Ok don't cry

Y/n- emoma please come with me Y/m laughed And said -Y/n. I can't come with u u are now married ok Jungkook will take a good care of u ok Said kissing your forehead.

Mr Jeon -Ok Miss y/m we should go now

Y/m nod Y/n-Emoma i will come tomorrow don't cry

Y/m laughed and nod

Soon they reach the Jeon mansion

The house was damm big There were maid standing there line by line We waked inside the house Everyone bowed.

We sat into the couch Mr jeon -So everyone She is your new queen our Jungkook wife's

Everyone bowed there head towards u .

Jungkook -Dad i have to go somewhere Mrs jeon But son it's late in night and today is your wedding night where re u going

Jungkook -Mom i have something important to deal with

Mr Jeon -Ok u better came back soon.

Jungkook nod and made a eyes contract with u But soon he broke the eye contact And he left from hereMrs jeon -Y/n daughter he had something important don't worry he will come back ok Y/n nod slightly.Mr jeon -Ok y/n daughter u should take some rest Mrs jeon -One of our members our very trusted maid wil show u everything ok Mrs jeon -Maria go and show there bedroom Maria -Yes mam come with me Said bowing her head They walked inside the room It was beautiful, gorgeous, large bed (ifukuk) Maria -Mam if u need anything just call me ok Y/n nod Maria left Y/nWalked to the balcony Thinking about what did she do Did she do correct? Or wrong?She kept the thinking aside and walked to bathroom To take shower After 30min she came Wearing night dress She was applied creamThan The door Suddenly oPEN Only toSee jungkook standing there in drunk

Chapter 28

Jungkook Have been Standing There in Drunk.

I slowly stand up from the dressing table chair.

It was a quiet silent just breath can be heard and soon the raining started...No words. Just staring at each other with hate, anger, frustration...

He walked towards me his waking can be heard hard.Waking towards me the step he takes towards me .. I take step back..Not knowing the Wall hit my back...

He came towards me so close that my heartbeat can be heard..He observed my face seeing the reaction i hold for him ...

He said in his deep voice...I don't.. know what happened that time.i don't know why .. Olivia ran away but . The thing is I'm not going to see u as I see to Oliva.

Those words break my heart i don't know why but the pain i felt in my heart no one could ever.

Jungkook said again with his deep voice.Y/n.. so don't feel anything towards me u are just my a name--Called --wife noting els e.As u know tomorrow many people will come for our marriage event my friends my mafia friends just act we are in so-- called.love nothing else.

He walked towards the bed sitting on it He opened his tshirt and his shoes and step into the bed laiding on it .

He said..Are u going to look me with those eyes or try to sleep.In the couch

Y/n pov -Me! In the couch i have never ever sleep in the couch and he wants me to this idiot! Jungkook

Y/n said.. i... Don't sleep in the couch in my life u sleep in the....--couch.

Jungkook laughed and said...U want Jungkook the mafia leader the most feared man to sleep in the couch for my sooo--called .wife. no liltle princess never.

Y/n said.... I don't know if u are a most feared man i don't know but I'm not going to sleep in the couch......

Jungkook said...Either u are going to sleep in couch or ...In the bed with me princess.

Y/n pov --It was raining to hard and it was cold I can't sleep in couch but emoma said that he is my husband i can do whatever I don't have to feel shy i can sleep in bed with him but we are not doing it right!?Yes right..

Jungkook observed her reaction thinking and thinking about what she is going to do

Jungkook said... Princess are u Coming in bed or in the couch

Y/n said I'm ... C--oming in bed

She laid on the bed closing her eyes Jungkook turned the light off Just the morning came soon.....

The Bird singing there lovely song softly..The weather was perfect for the day...

Chapter 29

Party. Party yay.= 29 Mafia professor Jeon.

The Bird singing there lovely song A good weather

Jk pov -I slowly opened my eye the sunshine came towards my eyes.. i sat up on the bed Feeling a heavy weight on my legs Not one and only but my so-called wife' putting her leg in my legs (wow good starting)

Jk _ hey.. wake up u hey u ...Said trying to pull her leg away from him

Y/n pov -Someone's was pulling me who the hell is ittt ?not knowing it was my faithfully Mr Jeon Jungkook idiot my hus band.Not knowing he fell down in the floor!

Jk pov -Suddenly I fell down in the floor because of my so-called wife' y/n pushed me in her sleep what a great morning.

Jungkook _- what the hell is wrong with u y/n.Said in gridding teeth.

Y/n_- i .. d--id t do anything

Jungkook _- oh really than how am I in down answer me .

Jungkook -u dare- suddenly my phone rang.My friend tae called me .

I accept the call Jungkook - why did u called me in the dam Morning.

V- ohh bro calm down did I disturb something said laughing

Jungkook.- disturb something stop with this nothing happened and never

V- while how is my y/n

Jungkook - sleeping in my bed and she pushed me in sleep what the hell is wrong with her.

V- he couldn't say anything but started laughing sooo hard.

Jungkook cut the call.

Y/n- are u happy now doing me embarrassing with your friend . Said with a pout.

Jungkook - yes I'm

Time skip after there little bit fight....

It was time for the newlyweds party.

The maid was helping her makeup artist everything

Y/n outfit=

Mrs jeon entered the room'

Mrs jeon - u are looking sooo gorgeous y/n

Y/n bowed her head. As a thankyou.

The maid said Mrs jeon mr Jeon said to come down people are waiting.

Mrs jeon Ok

She looked at u .

Come on y/n let's go down people are waiting for u right.

The venue

Jungkook was standing and taking with his Mafia friends.

Jungkook outfit

Jungkook eyes laid on y/n waking down'Jungkook pov=They way she walks in she is looking dam fucking gorgeous i didn't saw her like that before fuck it's making me hard damm hard.!.

Chapter 30

Reception party.

Jungkook POV The way she walks in she is looking dam fucking gorgeous i didn't saw her like that before Fuck! It's making me hard .

His friends wisped how beautiful Jungkook is boos wife is .

Everyone sat at there respective chair .Mrs jeon and mr Jeon was in the stage While Jungkook and y/n were standing together.

Y/n her breath was going High she never felt so many people and those are all Mafia people dangerous.

Jungkook see this and softly wisped into her ear Princess keep breathing I'm with u my so-called wife'.

Y/n touched her chest calming herself down.

Soon mr Jeon gave a speech.

Ahmh. Good evening everyone thanks for coming for my son Jeon Jungkook weeding reception party. As well her name is y/n jeon she is going to be your queen from now on.

Y/n became shocked.

ButJungkook smirk.

Soon they finished.And everyone started doing injoyingThemselves mr and mrs Jeon (Jungkook mom dad who is thinking something else let me clear them thanks.)

Jungkook and y/n was standing in the stage there friends talking with them.

Soon kim taehyung came.Taehyung outfit

. taehyung came towards them he slightly smiled at y/n .

Happy marriage for both of u Said giving a gift to y/n

Jungkook u didn't told me the story how u accept this replacement bride He wisped to Jungkook so only Jungkook can heard.

Jungkook was about to say but suddenly his one of childhood friends called him Taehyung I'm coming stay with y/n don't let anyone touch her .

He said and looking to you for a second then waking to his friends

Y/n what a destiny right. I thought to marry u but the destiny wants u to marry Jungkook .Taehyung said with a hurtful smirk.

I---..am forced.. but .. I believe in God.. whatever he did.. he did for good..Y/n said.

Y/n forget it..why don't u enjoy there are many drinks come on Taehyung said pulling her to alcohol large variety drink

Taehyung... I don't-- drink....Said

Y/n don't be a kid enjoy He said giving a drink to y/n

I don't drink... please try -- t--o understand.

Author.Taehyung forcefully gave the drink Y/n drank it .She can feel her head spinning

Can I have more .Said in drunk voice cuz she never drank in her life of course if you drink first time the most expensive it will make u drunk by one glass

Chugging down the another drink not aware of the widen eyes taehyung watching u with terror and before u couch say anything.

Jungkook said!- WHAT THE HELL ARE U DRINKING!

! Your body freeze your hand shaking Jungkook large hands was around your arm. Holding u in a firm grip without hurting much.

Taehyung just stand there nervous scared of his life.

Who gave u this drink y/n Jungkook said still holding her arms

I pointed to taehyung.

Taehyung eye widened in scared.

Taehyung u! Jungkook said

Jungkook.. wiat listen... Wait . Wait .....I gave her a drink because it was your wedding function i thought she will enjoy i didn't know that only form one glass she will get drunk ... T--tust me .Taehyung said in one breath.

She haven't drink in her life.Jungkook shouted to taehyung And music was louder so nobody can hear it

Y/n slowly laid her head in Jungkook shoulder

Jungkook saw this and he carried her in bridal style.

Tell to mom that she was not feeling well so she went to her room.Jungkook said and waked upstairs to there bedroom.

He opened by his leg the door and put her on the bed he closed the door.

He walked towards her and sat beside Watching her innocence face sleeping

He slowly pushed her hair in from her face clearly watching her face

U slowly say something in wisped in sleep

Ju..gkook idiot.. i like u secretly but not wanting to tell u at your scary face... please believe me i didn't do anything She wisped she was drunk she doesn't know what she was saying U slowly opened your eyes

Jung-kook please believe.. me i didn't do anything i didn't even know where Oliva went please trust... M_-e Y/n said her tear slowly came

Autor pov-Jungkook heart felt pain he can't see u like that but before he saw many people crying many girls but he never felt pain in his heart watching u crying

He slowly reached his hand tumb to wiped your tears

S.top crying . Said softly To u .

Suddenly y/n hug Jungkookkk Jungkook warped his hand towards your waist u buried your face into his chest

I don't know what I'm to u a replacement bride. Or a bride.Y/n said crying.

Stop crying y/n u are my wife u understand u are my wife Jungkook softly kiss your forehead

Y/n opened her eyes she looks to Jungkook Can u .. fu--ck me... Jungkook.

Chapter 31

Jungkook....can u fu--ck me.I said to him desire in my eyes for him to fuck me tonight.

Author POV Jungkook didn't understand but his Hard cock almost punched a hold though his pants,And the image is running in his mind

Y/n u sure u wanna do it Said holding her hand

Y-es please..

Author POV (Jungkook)

Fuck. I was going to destroy her but, i can't hold it back anymore

He stands up he said "Take of your clothes"

Y/n (u) she didn't hesitate. She unzipped her dress it fell on the floor.

Her skin glowed benid the red dress she was wearing it's on the floor her body.. shit. Her round ass, long leg,the cute liltle pussy, Her rosy nipples that were perfect for sucking one and only me "jeon Jungkook"

She stared at me knowing i will not hurt herHer sweet big brown eyes.

I stand towards her she was standing our body touching her nacked boday was. A dam wish to be fuck her.

Jungkook pressed his lip to your neck "

Y/n u want me to ruin u ?

Y--es.

Jungkook licked the hollow between your neck and lower jaw .

He striped his clothes off and came up behind her already she was laiding in bed he spread her things with his hands.

You are wet y/n aren't u He said kicking her glistening juice off her skin He pushed a finger inside her tight, slick folds and was rewarded with a loud moaned her u

Princess u want me to fuck u Said in soft voice

Y--es please jungk-ook .

He found the spot that had her bucking against her face he gently tugg his mouth in your clit with his teeth with his tongue Y/n scream loudly

Princess i promise I will be gentle

He get his cock inside her pussy

She scream The blood little came out

Jungkook notice He kissed her forehead

After 1 hours

They finally finished. He clean y/n and they were in bed in Jungkook arms he was hugging her

Soon they fall asleep

Chapter 32

They soon slept in each other arms Bet u know Jungkook is in love with y/n (u)

Author POV Y/n was drunk but that doesn't mean she was a little bit aware to know it was Jungkook No matter what if it was another person she would kill him unlike it's her husband Jungkook.

Soon the morning came....

Author POV Y/n was still sore about the night of course it was her first time it will take long enough to get yourself in your head as well Meanwhile Jungkook He is sitting and admiring his beautiful wife y/nWho is sleeping peacefully with a little pout in her lips Doe eyes, juicy lips, no matter Jungkook couldn't Hold himself and he softly kiss her cheek While the party went fine like a euphoria Mrs Jeon mr Jeon was happy after taehyung Said he took take care of y/n and Jungkook was angry because of drunk she went and The parents felt really happy too saw them with each other they know it is a force marriage for y/n Jungkook didn't even know that Oliva went out telling she doesn't love Jungkook {But the destiny is what u it is now can't help but consider a life that can live with}

Y/n slowly opened her eyes due to the softly kiss Morning darling Jungkook said softly to her cuz it was her day after the night went

Mr idiot Jungkook why are u sleeping with me Y/n said in her baby voice

I--- y/n eyes went to her body seeing only in tshirt her legs were paining

H--ow I'm nacked... Jungkook how I'm nacked did i do with someone!? Jungkook or it is u Y/n said nervously scared, if she had s** with a stranger person

Darling u are safe it was me your husband darling y/n Jungkook said softly touching her neck

It was me and I'm going to be your very last darling Said in deep voice, can give u shivers in your body

Author POV Jungkook explained everything how they had.Y/n understand.

Y/n.. im really sorry about the behaviour i did with u and I'm totally aware now last night u said u don't know how Olivia went u are sorry about it but it is not your fault y/n i understand now please I know the times can' t Come back but the future we are holding now. Is (u and me .) y/n.. can u give us a chance about this marriage i promise I I will never ever do like that behaviour with u i promise sweetheart will u give us a chance...?

Y/n couldn't hold back her tears because now he understands that it's not her fault Now she cant do anything unlike she didn't have any boyfriend or something or a crush Now it was him who is her future Jeon Jungkook her husband, her future. She can give a chance to this marriage but mom dad are free that y/n is married to Jungkook of course every parent would want her daughter to marry a person billionaire gentleman but Jungkook was hard but deep down' he needed someone to bring the sweetness in his body and now he have her.

Yes.. Jungkook let's give a try to the marriage Y/n said. With her real feelings

Jungkook hugged y/n tightly closely to him The love they are having now is in another level

Chapter 33

POV y/n-

I have been spending time with my mr stupid Jeon jungkook my husband of course u know about it .. and the night I have lose my virginity I knew that jungkook and I were in love. Cute right... So from that day I got to spend time with him u know and his parents were sooo nice and his parents is my parents too and I have been feeling something in my stomach..

It was morning..

The room was pleased with birds singing cutely jungkook and y/n hugging each other were sleeping they were in love for sure .

Suddenly y/n opened her eyes andShe pushed jungkook and runnnnn too bathroom..

Jungkook lain in floor with a tump Hahahaa... And u know what can happen

Jungkook followed y/n inside the bathroom and y/n was vomiting

Jungkook knew that something was wrong with her ..Because of potato I guess because u doesn't like potato

And y/n eat yesterday from yesterday she is feeling vomiting and y/n thinks this But for jungkook he thinks somethingI guess the reader knew what I'm talking aboutHehe

Jungkook povY/n u are coming with me to doctor we will check about your healthAnd we will go right now.

I said in my serious voice because I know if it is this than it is .

Time skip to doctor.

Hi mr Jeon and Mrs Jeon I have a good news

Yes!? Jungkook and u said

U guys are going to be parents!!!

What!!!!! Jungkook shouted in happiness

- im- pregnant-- Y/n said with tears happy tears

Yes Mrs Jeon congratulations!

ThankyouJungkook said and y/n

Y/n I love u thankyou for giving me a special gift omg I can't wait to hold our BBY

Jungkook I love u tooo

I love u more y/n

End